ZAYDO POTATO
A Muslim
SUPERHERO

BY RANDA TAFTAF & MAZ GALINI
ILLUSTRATED BY LOVYAA GARG

We dedicate this story

to every child who loves superheroes.

And, of course, we dedicate this story

to our very own Raya Amaraya.

We love you!

Auntie Randa and Uncle Maz

Rummana Publishing Inc.
PO Box 354
Riverview, FL 33568, USA
www.rummanapublishing.com
Library of Congress Control Number: 2017919133
Rummana Publishing Inc., Riverview, FL
ISBN 978-0999061046

Narrated by Abdullah bin Umar,
Prophet Mohammed PBUH said,
"A Muslim is a brother of another Muslim, so he should not oppress him, nor should he hand him over to an oppressor. Whoever fulfilled the needs of his brother, Allah (swt) will fulfill his needs; whoever brought his (Muslim) brother out of a discomfort, Allah will bring him out of the discomforts of the Day of Resurrection, and whoever screened a Muslim, Allah will screen him on the Day of Resurrection."

-Sahih Bukhari

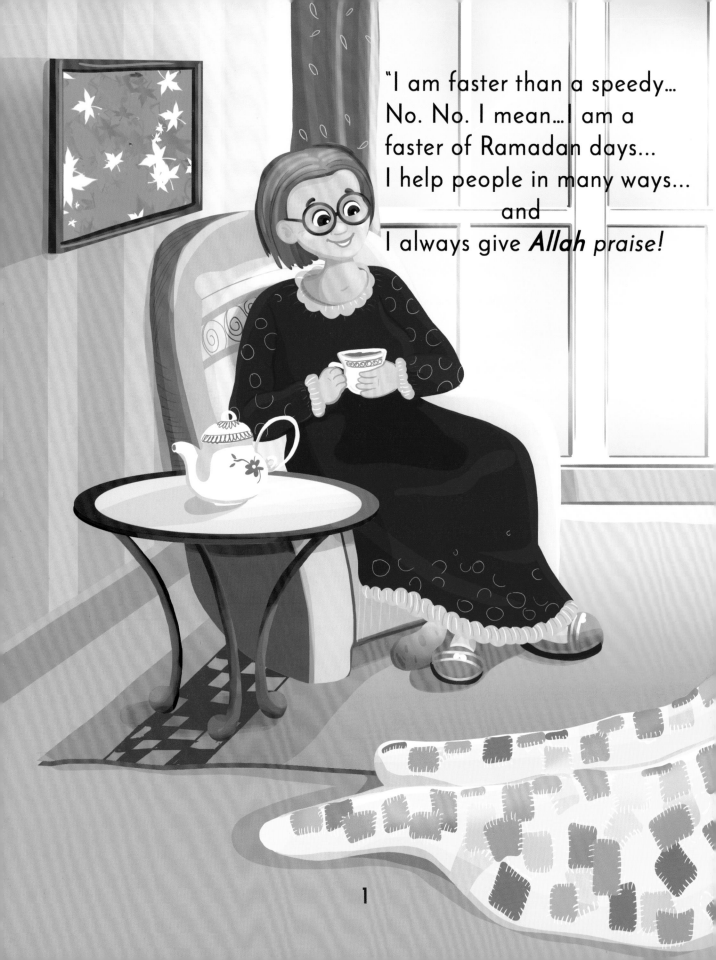

"I am faster than a speedy...
No. No. I mean...I am a
faster of Ramadan days...
I help people in many ways...
and
I always give **Allah** praise!

"I am Super Zaydo Potato, a Muslim Superhero, and this is my loyal and spicy sidekick **Black Pepper!**"

2

"Oh, Super Zaydo Potato, can I be a Muslim superhero, too?" asked Raya.

"Of course!" replied Super Zaydo. "The world is definitely in need of more **Muslim superheroes!**"

"But I don't know how to be a Muslim superhero," replied Raya sadly.

"DON'T WORRY, Raya!
There's a superhero inside each one of us.
Black Pepper and I will show you,"
said Super Zaydo Potato.

4

"Black Pepper and I are always on the lookout for anyone in need of help!" said Super Zaydo Potato.

"How do you do that?" asked Raya.

5

"We use our super senses," explained Super Zaydo.
"Waaaaaa!"
**"Did you hear that? Someone is in distress!
Let's hurry to the rescue!"**
exclaimed Super Zaydo.

6

"Never fear! The Muslim Superheroes are here!"
"What's wrong, Salma?" asked Raya.

"Our jump rope broke!"cried Salma.

"Don't worry! Here's a brand new rope just for you." said Super Zaydo.

7

"Oh, no! You gave away your super belt! How are you going to be a superhero now?" exclaimed Raya

"The girls needed that belt more," answered Super Zaydo.

8

"Look out, Omar!" screamed Raya.
"Never fear! The Muslim Superheroes are here!"
"Are you okay, Omar?" asked Raya.

"Ouch! My arm hurts," whined Omar.

"Don't worry, Omar! **Soon**, you'll be as good as new **Insha'Allah**," said Super Zaydo Potato as he wrapped Omar's arm in a sling.

"Oh, no! You gave away your secret identity! How are you going to be a superhero now?" exclaimed Raya.

"Omar needed that bandana more," answered Super Zaydo Potato.

"What's that noise? Let's follow that sound!" exclaimed Super Zaydo
Shhhh!" It's just Grandpa's **SNORING**," whispered Super Zaydo Potato.

11

"Oh, no! You gave away your cape and shield! How are you going to be a Superhero now?" grumbled Raya.

"Grandpa **needed** my cape more," whispered Super Zaydo Potato.

"**Waaaaa!**" Baby Haya cried from the next room.

"Never fear! The Muslim Superheroes are here!
There, there, Haya, don't cry.
I have something that
I'm sure will make
you smile."

Zaydo takes off his super gloves and...
exclaims "Look, Haya, it's a bunny!"

13

"Oh, no! You gave away your super punching gloves!
How are you going to be a superhero now?"
exclaimed Raya, then continued "Don't answer that.
I know, I know. Haya needed those gloves more!"

"Noooo, Black Pepper! Watch out!"

Raya immediately took off her towel cape and placed it over the puddle. "There! Now no one will slip on the water and get hurt!" exclaimed Raya.

"*Bravo, Raya! You are now officially* **Super Raya Amaraya!** Our costumes don't give us superpowers or make us superheroes! Like **YOU**, superheroes **always** put others first," said Super Zaydo.

"That's right,
Super Raya and **Super Zaydo.**
I made you these **super special**
superhero costumes just to keep
your secret identities **safe**,"
winked Grandma.

18

Dear Parents,
Thank you for purchasing this book! As a thank you, we've included some suggestions to make this story even more fun, educational, and engaging. The activities below are designed to help your child master different skills such as counting, matching, recognizing shapes, phonics, and more! As you and your child read, you will probably come up with your own fun activities to enjoy and share. Happy reading!
Love,
Randa and Maz

COUNTING

Can you count the number of items in
Super Zaydo Potato's makeshift costume?
Super Raya's makeshift costume?

SHAPES

Go to pages 11-12 and ask your child to find and point out the following shapes:
-circle
-square
-triangle

PHONICS

Zaydo, Raya, and Pepper love being superheroes! Can you find words or objects in the story that begin with the letters
S-U-P-E-R-H-E-R-O-E-S

SPATIAL RELATIONS

Where are Pepper and the hidden potato in every page? Ask your child to use words such as
-over
-under
-behind
-next to

CRITICAL THINKING

Search for Grandma in the story. What do you think Tete is doing in each spread?

Did you enjoy this story?

We hope you did! Check out *Zaydo Potato: Allah Loves Me* and *Zaydo Potato: Can Allah See Me Now?* for more Zaydo Potato fun. Salams!

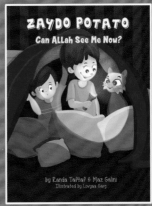

Rummana Publishing Inc
Educate·Empower·Inspire

Rummana Publishing is dedicated to educate and provide quality Arabic as a foreign language resources, empower young Muslims with collections of children's books with Muslim characters, and inspire more (but not limited to) Arab and Muslim writers to write and spread love and understanding.
For more fun material visit us at www.rummanapublishing.com

About the Authors:

RANDA TAFTAF
Founder of Rummana Publishing
Randa is a bilingual, Syrian-American born in Youngstown, Ohio. She grew up in Pennsylvania and moved to Damascus, Syria at the age of 14. She now lives in Florida with her husband and son Zayd.

Equipped with a fiery passion for languages and an MEd in Foreign Language Education, Randa is a seasoned foreign language instructor of 17 years and counting. Over the course of her career, she has managed and led exemplary ESL programs, actively trained ESL instructors, developed a curriculum for the teaching of Arabic as a Second Language and much more. As an American of Syrian heritage, she strives to bridge the cultures of the east and west through education and storytelling both inside and outside her classrooms and even in her own home. Consequently, she founded Rummana Publishing Inc. with her husband Maz to educate, empower and inspire.
Follow her work on Instagram and Twitter @rummanapublishing

MAZ GALINI
Co-Founder of Rummana Publishing
Maz is a Lebanese-American polyglot. Fluent in four languages: English, Arabic, French, and Spanish, Maz can step inside the mind and context of other cultures easily. Maz prefers to connect cultures and express himself more creatively through his work as a web designer/developer in additon to his writing and exceptional photography. Sharing in the vision to educate, empower and inspire his son Zayd and future generations, Maz co-founded Rummana Publishing Inc. with his wife, Randa.
Follow Maz's work on Instagram @mazgalini and check out his page www.mazgalini.com